Dad Jokes
& CARTOONS

reviews

AMAZON REVIEWS ARE APPRECIATED!

designerinkbooks@gmail.com

Copyright © 2022 DESIGNER INK

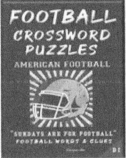

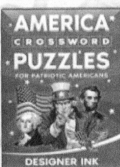

CONTENTS

Chapter One DAD JOKES 1

Chapter Two SPORTS JOKES 17

Chapter Three DUMB GUY JOKES 30

Chapter Four DAD JOKES #2 40

Chapter Five CLEAN JOKES 56

Chapter Six DUMB GUY JOKES #2 74

Chapter Seven DAD JOKES #3 86

Chapter Eight CORNY JOKES 104

Chapter Nine DUMB GUY JOKES #3 114

Chapter Ten SUPER JOKES 126

Chapter Eleven YUK-YUK JOKES 140

Chapter Twelve MORE CARTOONS 156

Har!
Har!
Har!

Chapter One

DAD JOKES

Chapter One - Dad Jokes

DENTIST

Q: What's the problem with eating a clock?

A: It's time-consuming.

CONSTRUCTION

Lance: "Tell me your joke about construction."

Terry: "I can't because I'm still working on it."

BOSS

Q: Why did the guy get fired from his calendar factory job?

A: Because he took a couple of days off.

Chapter One - Dad Jokes

CAT

Kathy: "Dad, can you put the cat out?"

Dad: "I didn't even know the cat was on fire."

ELON MUSK

Q: Have you heard what the mainstream media is calling the new Elon Musk controversy?

A: "Elon-Gate."

Seems like a bit of a stretch.

TIME

Lanny: "What time is it?"

Rex: "I don't know. It keeps changing."

APPLE STORE

Q: What do you become after you see a robbery at an Apple Store???

A: An iWitness?

Chapter One - Dad Jokes

VEGAS, BABY. VEGAS

Q: Which Nevada city do dentists visit the most?

A: Floss Vegas

TRIMMED

Jimmie: "Are you thinking about getting a new haircut?"

Manny: "Yes, but I'm going to mullet over first."

SHOES

Patty: "John, can you put my shoes on?"

John: "I can try, but I don't think they're going to fit me."

MERGED PACKAGES

Q: Did you hear about the possible merger between FedEx & UPS?

A: From now on, they'll be known as "Fed-Up."

Chapter One - Dad Jokes

AVERAGE

Dale: "My friend said I was just average."

Nancy: "I think he's mean."

FISH

Q: What kind of fish has two knees?

A: A two-knee fish! Yuk yuk

CALL ME

Karl: "I'll call you later."

George: "Don't call me later. Call me George."

ACTRESS INJURY

Herbert: Did you hear the news of the famous actress that was hurt on that cooking show?

Georgina: "Oh, no. Who?"

Herbert: "Hmmmm, it might be Reese something?"

Georgina: "Witherspoon???"

Herbert: "No, it was with a knife."

Chapter One - Dad Jokes

HIPSTER

Q: How did the hipster drown?

A: In the mainstream.

ARROW

Frank: "Time flies like an arrow."

Halie: "And fruit flies like a banana."

SPACE EATERY

Q: What is good and bad about that restaurant on Mars?

A: It has really great food, but no atmosphere.

ARK

Larry: "Do you need an ark?"

Perry: "Why?"

Larry: "Because I Noah guy!"

Chapter One - Dad Jokes

CANNED

Q: What do you call cans of food that eat other cans of food?

A: CANnibals.

CAKE

Abby: "Johnny, make me a cake!"

Johnny: "Abracadabra, you're a cake!"

ARTIST

Q: Did you hear what happened to the missing comic book artist?

A: The details are sketchy at this time.

NOODLE

Herb: "What do you call a fake noodle?"

Larry: "I don't know. What?"

Herb: "An Impasta. Ha-ha"

Chapter One - Dad Jokes

INVISIBLE

Q: Why did the invisible woman turn down the new job offer?

A: She just couldn't see herself doing it.

CLOWNS

A couple of cannibals are eating a circus clown when one of them says to the other: "Does this taste funny to you?"

MODERATION

Q: Did you hear about the new store named "Moderation"?

A: I guess they have everything in there.

GOLDFISH

A couple of goldfish are in a tank. One fish says to the other fish,

"Hey, do you know how to drive this thing?"

Chapter One - Dad Jokes

INVISIBLE FAMILY

Q: Have you heard about the invisible man marrying the invisible woman and starting a family?

A: It turns out the kids are nothing to look at.

GRAVEYARD

Q: Why is the local graveyard so darn overcrowded?

A: Because people are dying to get in.

OK, BOSS

My supervisor told me to have a great day.

So I went home. Ha-ha

NUMBERS

Q: What did the number 0 say to the number 8?

A: Nice belt!

Chapter One - Dad Jokes

BEAVERS

Wendy: "What's your opinion on the TV show about beavers?

Lorne: "It is the best dam show on TV today."

WAITING

Restaurant greeter: "Sorry about your wait."

Customer: "Hey, are you implying I'm fat?"

Chapter One - Dad Jokes

MOVIES

Last weekend my friend and I viewed 2 movies back-to-back.

Fortunately, I was the one facing the screen.

COFFEE

Q: Why did the coffee visit the police station?

A: Because it was mugged.

NINJA

James: "What has 2 butts & has killed people?"

Percy: "I don't know. What?"

James: "An assassin."

HOTDOG

A hotdog strolls into a bar.

The bartender says: "Unfortunately, we don't serve food here."

Chapter One - Dad Jokes

BRRRRRR

Q: How does a citizen of the North Pole build their house?

A: Igloos it together.

PIRATE

Q: What does a swash-buckling pirate say on his 80th birthday?

A: "AYE, MATEY"

THE GREAT

Q: Where did Alexander The Great keep his armies?

A: Up his sleevies!

CARS

Q: What's the name of a Mexican that has lost his car?

A: Carlos.

SWISS

Q: What is the greatest thing about living in Switzerland?

A: I have no idea, but their flag is a big plus.

LEFTY

Q: Did you hear the news about the woman who had her entire left side cut off?

A: She's all right now!

SKELETONS

Q: Why do skeletons never ever go out trick 'or' treating?

A: Because skeletons have no body to go out with.

SIREN

A man on the street sees an ambulance raced by at top speed with its siren going off.

"They won't sell any ice-cream if they keep driving that fast."

LOGS

Darcy: "Yawn. I slept like a log last night."

Jamie: "Did you wake up in the fireplace?"

ELEPHANT

Q: What do you call an elephant that nobody cares about???

A: An irrelephant

FOUNDING FATHER

I told my friend I was named after George Washington.

She said, "I thought your name was Brian."

And I said, "It is Brian, but I was named AFTER George Washington."

RUBBER TOE

Oliver: "What do you call the man with the rubber toe?"

Samuel: "I don't know. What?"

Oliver: "Roberto!"

MAGIC

Q: What breed of dog can perform magic tricks?

A: A L-abracadabra-dor.

Chapter Two

SPORTS JOKES

PAINTBALL

Q: Why is paintball the most violent sport?

A: It involves a lot of dyeing.

BOOMERANG

I had forgotten how to throw a boomerang....

But after a while, it came back to me.

ARCHERY

Frank: "Have you tried that new sport of blindfold archery?"

George: "No, I haven't."

Frank: "You don't know what you're missing."

CANUCKS

Q: Why are Canadians so great at hockey?

A: Because they always bring their 'eh' game

GOLF GAMBLING

2 buddies were out golfing. The first golfer likes to gamble, so he says to his friend....

Golfer #1: "How about we make it interesting. $1 a hole, $10 for the winner of the front 9, $10 for the back 9, and $100 for holes in 1?"

Golfer #2 agrees, steps up to the 1st tee, and nails a hole in 1.

Golfer #1, potentially down $100 says unfazed:

Golfer #1: "Great, now I will take MY practice shot, then we can get started."

Chapter Two – Sports Jokes

OH, WAITER

Husband: "Excuse me, waiter, my wife spilled her drink."

Waiter: "No problem, sir, I'll get you a replacement one right away."

Husband: "Any chance the next one likes sports?"

PASS

Bill B: "Did you hear they're giving away former Seahawk Marshawn Lynch jerseys at Sport Depot. We should go get one.

Pete C.: "I think I'll pass."

VIDEOGAMES

EA Sports - It's in the game.

Just kidding, it's in the game's patch, DLC, or next year's game.

SKIING

Some people love the sport of skiing...

But that sport is going downhill, really fast.

RACKET

Q: What is the most popular time to play a racket sport?

A: Ten-ish.

TROPHIES

I used to play all types of sports but never won at anything.

Then I realized I could buy trophies.

Now I'm good at everything. Ha-ha

Chapter Two – Sports Jokes

FRENCH

Me: Do you play any type of sport?

French person: Wii

NOISE

Q: What is the noisiest sport?

A: Racketball (racquetball)

BADDY

Q: Which racket sport is a troublemaker?

A: BADminton.

DONUTS

Your uncle Ned is so dumb that he thought Dunkin' Donuts was a pro basketball team.

Chapter Two – Sports Jokes

SUPER BOWL

It's Super Bowl Sunday, and a young man makes his way down to his seat. The man notices the seat next to him is empty. He asks an older gentleman on the other side of the empty seat if anyone is sitting there.

Older Gentleman: "There's nobody sitting there."

Young Man: "That's crazy. Someone doesn't show up for Super Bowl?"

Older Gentleman: "The seat is my wife's, but she passed away. We've been to every Super Bowl since we got married. This is the first time we aren't together for the game."

Young Man: "I'm sorry to hear that. Weren't there any friends or relatives that could have taken the seat?"

Older Gentleman: "No, they're all at the funeral."

IMPROVING

Golfer: "I believe my game is improving?"

Caddy: "I agree. You miss the ball much closer now."

PANTS

Q: "Why do golfers often wear two pairs of pants?"

A: In case they get a hole in one. Ha-ha

DRINKS

Q: What type of tea do ice hockey players drink?

A: Penal-tea

Chapter Two – Sports Jokes

MISCOMMUNICATION

For 2 weeks in a row, my son and I were the only people to show up for his team's football practice. Frustrated, I said to my son,

Father: "Son, please tell your coach that I'm upset that only we showed up for this week's practice yet again."

Son: Rolling his eyes, "He'll just say the same thing he told me last time."

Father: "Which was what?"

Son: "That he told everyone that practice is now on Fridays, not Thursdays.

MADNESS

Q: What did the month of March say to the madness?

A: "What's all that bracket?"

Chapter Two – Sports Jokes

TEST

The School's Hockey coach entered the locker room prior to game time, sat next to the star player and said….

Coach: "I'm not allowed to play you because you failed your math exam. But the principal agreed to let you play if you can answer correctly 1 simple math question."

Star Player: "OK, coach. I'll try."

Coach: "Take your time, concentrate, think…..what is 2 + 2?"

The star player thinks long and hard and answers….

Star Player: "is it 4?"

Coach: "Did you say 4?!?" He exclaimed and started shouting and running around

Several teammates: "Ah, c'mon, coach…. give the poor guy another chance!"

Chapter Two – Sports Jokes

OLYMPICS

Q: Why has suntanning never qualified as an Olympic sport?

A: Because the best anyone can ever get is bronze.

TEA BAG

Peter: What's the difference between Team England and a tea bag?

Jarred: "I don't know. What?"

Peter: A teabag can stay in the cup much longer.

CLIMBING

Samuel: "Any advice for me regarding my stair climbing competition?"

Larry: There are a lot of good climbers in the contest. You'd better step up your game."

Chapter Two – Sports Jokes

JUNGLE CAT

Q: Why was the jungle cat banned from the race?

A: Because he's a known Cheetah.

POLITICS

Dale: "What's the difference between politics and baseball?"

Harry: "I don't know. What?"

Dale: "In baseball, you're out when you're caught stealing."

Chapter Two – Sports Jokes

STADIUM

Q: Why did it get so hot in the stadium after the soccer game?

A: Because all the fans left.

Chapter Three

DUMB GUY JOKES

Chapter Three – Dumb Guy Jokes

SUBMARINE

Q: How do you sink a dumb guy's submarine?

A: Just knock on the door.

BIRDY

Q: How did the dumb guy attempt to kill the bird?

A: He threw it off a cliff.

Chapter Three – Dumb Guy Jokes

MIRROR, MIRROR

Q: Why were there a lot of bullet holes in the mirror?

A: Because a dumb guy tried to shoot at an identity thief.

SNOWMAN

Q: Why does it take so darn long to construct a dumb guy snowman?

A: Because you have to hollow out the brain area.

HOLE

Two dumb guys fell down into a deep hole.

Dumb guy #1: "It sure is dark down here, isn't it?"

Dumb guy #2: "I don't know; I can't see."

Chapter Three – Dumb Guy Jokes

HUH?

Q: What can strike a dumb guy without him even knowing?

A: A thought.

JUICE

Q: How come the dumb guy stared intently at the frozen juice can for 3 hours?

A: Because the label read "concentrate."

RAKING

Q: How did the dumb guy sustain an injury while raking the leaves?

A: He fell out of the tree.

Chapter Three – Dumb Guy Jokes

WISHES

A dumb guy, and his 2 friends, Bob and Steve, were all lost in the forest.

They were desperate and nearly gave up all hope when they spotted a magic lamp.

When they rubbed it, a giant genie came out and said that he would grant 1 wish to each of them.

Bob told the genie that he wished he could return home to his family, and magically he was back home.

Steve told the genie he also wished to be with his family but wanted them all to be in Hawaii on the beach. Instantly, his wish was granted, and he was in Hawaii.

The genie turned to the dumb guy and asked him what he wanted. Then the dumb guy said, "I'm kinda lonely. I wish my friends were here."

Chapter Three – Dumb Guy Jokes

GRENADE

Harold: "What do you do when a dumb guy tosses a grenade at you?

Larry: "I don't know; what?"

Harold: "You pull the pin out and throw the grenade right back."

MEDICINE

Q: Why did the dumb guy sneak quietly past the medicine chest?

A: So he would not wake up the sleeping pills.

PAINTING

A dumb guy decided to paint the living room walls. When his wife came home, she asked him...

Wife: "Dear, why are you wearing both a leather coat as well as a winter coat at the same time?"

Dumb Guy: "The can label said, 'For best results, you need to apply 2 coats'."

Chapter Three – Dumb Guy Jokes

ROOF

Q: How do you get a dumb guy to go up on a roof?

A: Tell him that the drinks are on the house.

WATCH OUT

3 dumb guys walk into a bar.

You'd think at least 1 of them would've seen it.

Chapter Three – Dumb Guy Jokes

CROSS THE ROAD

2 dumb guys are standing facing each other across a road.

One dumb guy says to the other dumb guy,

Dumb Guy #1: "Hey, can I get to the other side?"

Dumb Guy #2: "What do you mean, you are already on the other side!"

HELP ME, DOC

A dumb guy visits a doctor's office.

The doctor asks the dumb guy,

Doctor: "What seems to be the problem?"

Dumb Guy: "Doc, my body hurts everywhere I touch it."

Doctor: "That can't be. Show me"

So the dumb guy proceeds to poke himself all over.

He pokes his arm "Ouch."

He pokes his leg "Ouch."

He pokes his stomach "Ouch."

Dumb Guy: "See, doc, it hurts everywhere."

After which, the doctor shakes his head in disbelief and says...

Doctor: "Your finger is broken."

Chapter Three – Dumb Guy Jokes

LIGHTS

Q: How can you get a dumb guy's eyes to light up?

A: Just shine a flashlight in his ears.

JOKES

Q: How do you make a dumb guy laugh on Sunday?

A: Tell him a joke on Thursday.

CONFUSION

Q: How do you confuse a dumb guy?

A: Place him in a circle, then tell him to go to the corner.

Chapter Three – Dumb Guy Jokes

COMPUTER

Q: Why did the dumb guy put soap & water on his computer?

A: He was trying to wash the Windows.

Chapter Four

DAD JOKES #2

CHEESE

Perry: "What do you call a chunk of cheese that isn't yours?"

Sara: "I don't know. What?"

Perry: "Nacho Cheese."

WORKING OUT

I went to a seafood gym yesterday.

Pulled a mussel!

CALENDAR

I worry for any calendar because its days are numbered.

GRAPE

Q: What happened to the grape when it was stepped on?

A: It let out a little wine.

DENTIST

Q: What time of day did your mom go to see the dentist?

A: Tooth hurt-y.

CLOCKS

Q: What did the hungry clocks do after finishing their buffet meals?

A: They went back four seconds.

VELCRO

Q: Why is it unwise to buy things that have velcro?

A: Because they are a complete rip-off.

OK?

Carlos: "Walter, are you alright."

Walter: "No, I'm half left."

SHOVEL IT

Q: What was said about the invention of the shovel?

A: That it was ground-breaking.

DUCK

2 men walked into a bar...

So the 3rd one ducked.

REMOTE CONTROL

Q: Why is the invention of the universal remote control so important to the TV industry?

A: Because it changed everything.

MILK

Grocery store worker: "Would you like the milk in a bag, miss?"

Miss: "No, please just leave it in the container!"

KIDDING

Q: When is a woman kidding?

A: When she's giving birth.

COP LINGO

Lawrence: "What did the cop say to the belly button?"

Parry: "I don't know. What?"

Lawrence: "You're under a vest!"

FRACTIONS

7/6 of all people say they're terrible with fractions.

BUFFALO

Q: What did the buffalo say to her son when she dropped him off at soccer practice?

A: "Bison."

NAPPING

Q: Did you hear the news about the kidnapping at the park?

A: It's ok. He woke up.

GIANT

Q: Have you heard the news about the giant that threw up?

A: It's all over town!

SHRIMP

Q: Why did the shrimp never share?

A: Because she was shellfish.

Chapter Four – Dad Jokes #2

PSYCHIC

Q: What do you call a chubby psychic?

A: A four-chin teller.

SUN

We stayed up all night long pondering where the sun had went...

Then it dawned on us.

SUSHI

Q: What's the one main problem with sushi???

A: It's a little fishy.

PEANUTS

Q: Did you hear what happened when the 2 peanuts were walking along the road?

A: One was a salted.

BUTTER

Q: Have you heard the rumor about the stick of butter?

A: Forget it. I really shouldn't spread it.

COW NAMES

Darren: "Do you know what you call a cow with only 2 legs?"

Harry: "No, what?"

Darren: "Lean beef."

Darren: "What if a cow has no legs?"

Harry: "I don't know, what?

Darren: "Ground beef."

SEAGULL

Q: What does one call a seagull that flies over a bay?

A: A bagel, of course.

EARTH

The complete rotation of the earth really completes my day.

ALMONDS

My girlfriend asked me to try that new all-almond diet everyone is talking about.

I said no, because that is just nuts.

COMPOSER

Q: What is the composer Beethoven's most favored fruit?

A: A ba-na-na-na.

BROWN

Q: What is not only brown but sticky?

A: A brown stick.

BANK IT

The United Kingdom doesn't have a kidney bank.

But it does have itself a Liverpool.

RANGE

Jim: "Do you want to come with me to the gun range?".

Greta: "Sure, I'll give it a shot!"

HORSE

Wally: "What did the horse shout after it fell down?"

Craig: "I don't know. What?"

Wally: "Help! I've fallen, and I can't giddyup!" Haha

Chapter Four – Dad Jokes #2

COLOR

Hank went to the doctor after ingesting some food coloring.

The doctor said he'd be ok, even though Hank felt like he dyed a little inside.

HIPPOS 'N' GO SEEK

Q: Why do you never ever see hippos hiding up in trees?

A: Because they're so darn good at it.

Chapter Four – Dad Jokes #2

STAIRS

Janice: "I don't trust stairs."

Peter: "why not?"

Janice: "Because I think they're always up to something."

NOISY PET

Q: What is the loudest pet of all?

A: A trumpet.

TRANSPLANT

Q: Did you hear about the old man that refused to get a brain transplant?

A: At the last minute, he changed his mind

SHOES

Q: What is the very worst thing about working inside a shoe recycling place?

A: It can be sole destroying.

PLANES

Q: What noise will a 747 make if it bounces?

A: Boeing, Boeing, Boeing. Haha

HAT RACK

2 hats were hanging on the hat rack.

One hat turns to the other hat and says, "You stay here. I'll go on a head". Har-dee-har-har

FLIPPING

Alice: "Did I tell you when I fell in love doing a backflip?"

Billy: "No. What happened?"

Alice: "I fell heels over head."

TIDE

Q: Is it easy to get ladies to avoid eating Tide pods?

A: I don't know. But it is more difficult to deter gents. Ha

Chapter Four – Dad Jokes #2

DONUTS

Q: Why on earth did the girl quit her donut factory job?

A: Because she was done with the hole business.

SOCCER

Q: Why do people play amateur soccer?

A: Just for kicks

FACTORY

Q: What do you call a factory that makes just average goods?

A: A satisfactory.

WINGS

David: "What do you call a fly with no wings?

Georgina: "I don't know. What?"

David: "A walk, of course."

GUITARS

A woman is in court for stealing a guitar collection.

The judge said, "First offender?"

She replied, "No, first it was a Gibson! Then a Fender."

CAT HEALTH

My cat puked today.

I don't think she's feline very well.

DIRECTIONS

My husband is really upset with me because I have no sense of direction.

So, I gathered my stuff and right!"

Chapter Five

CLEAN JOKES

Chapter Five – Clean Jokes

ALPHABET

John said: "I'm familiar with only 25 letters in the English alphabet....and I don't know why."

SHAPES

Q: What did the triangle say, meanly, to the circle?

A: "You know, you are pointless."

SQUIRREL

Q: How do you get a squirrel to want you?

A: Just act like a nut.

Chapter Five – Clean Jokes

CHOICES

Waiter: "Would you like a soup or salad, sir?"

Customer: "I don't want a SUPER salad. I just want a regular salad, please."

FUNNY

The comedian made apocalypse jokes like there was no tomorrow!

EGGS

Q: Why won't eggs tell each other any jokes?

A: Because they would crack each other up.

Chapter Five – Clean Jokes

FROSTY DRACULA

Q: What do you have if you mix a snowman and a vampire?

A: Frostbite.

GUMP

Q: What is Forrest Gump's log-in password?

A: 1forrest1

WHO?

Q: What do you call a person that has no body and no nose?

A: Nobody knows.

LOG IT

Lumberjack: "I've cut exactly 10,376 trees in my lifetime."

Kyle: "How do you know that?"

Lumberjack: "I keep a log."

Chapter Five – Clean Jokes

ELEVATOR

Q: Did you hear the positive story about the haunted elevator?

I guess it really raised a lot of spirits!

NOSEY

Dale: "Why can't a nose be 12" in length?"

Sally: "I don't know. Why?"

Dale: "Because then it'd be a foot."

Chapter Five – Clean Jokes

CHICKENS

Q: Why do chicken coops have just 2 doors?

Because the ones with 4 doors are called chicken sedans!

SODA

I had a nightmare that I was drowning in a huge ocean of orange soda.

When I awoke, I realized it was all just a Fanta Sea.

BOMBED

Q: How can you tell the comedian's chemistry joke bombed?

A: There's no reaction from the audience.

PENCIL

Q: What do you call a pencil with 2 erasers?

A: Pointless

Chapter Five – Clean Jokes

OCTOPUS

Q: How many tickles are required to make an octopus laugh out loud?

A: Ten tickles.

CHEESY

Q: How did the police interrogate the thief that stole a cheese sandwich?

A: They really grilled him.

SCARECROW

Harriet: "Do you know why the scarecrow deserved the award?"

Karen: "No. Why?"

Harriet: "Because he was outstanding in his field." Ha-ha-ha

Chapter Five – Clean Jokes

MAIL TIME

Q: What do you get when you mix up the letters of "Postmen."

A: Really ticked off postmen.

COWS

Q: What type of magic do dairy cows believe in?

A: Moodoo!

TISSUE

Anderson: "How do you get a tissue to dance?"

Julia: "I don't know. How?"

Anderson: "You blow a little boogie into it!"

Chapter Five – Clean Jokes

DOGGIE

Francis: "What did the 3-legged dog say to the bartender?"

Joseph: "I don't know. What?"

Francis: "I'm looking for the guy that shot my paw."

TOMATOES

Q: What did the slow-running tomato say to the other tomatoes?

A: "Don't worry about me. I'll ketchup."

GRAVITY

Q: What did the reviewer say about the anti-gravity book?

A: "This book is impossible to put down." Ha-ha

MUFFLER

Last night I had a nightmare that I was a muffler.

Then I woke up exhausted!

TELEVISION

Johnny: "Can I watch the television?"

Barbara: "Sure, just don't turn it on."

UNLOCK

Q: What type of key can never ever unlock a door?

A: A monkey

Chapter Five – Clean Jokes

KNOCK-KNOCKS

Q: Did you hear the news about the person who invented knock-knock jokes???

A: He won the 'no-bell' prize. Har-har-ha

SKELETON

Q: Why didn't the bony skeleton cross the road?

A: Because he didn't have the guts to do it!

VACUUM

My wife told me to sell our old vacuum cleaner.

It was just gathering dust!

BEARD

I never really liked having facial hair.

But then, all of a sudden it grew on me.

LIFESAVER

Q: How rich is the man that invented Lifesavers?

A: I don't know, but some say he made a mint.

WALLED

Taylor: "Do you know what the fish said when it swam right into a wall?"

Stacy: "No. What did it say?"

Taylor: "Damn!"

THE LAW

Q: Why did the sheriff make rounded bails of hay against the law in North Dakota?

A: Because the state cows were not getting a square meal.

Chapter Five – Clean Jokes

MUSIC

Q: What kind of music does the group called 'Cellophane' perform?

A: They mostly wrap.

CHEESE, SHHH

Karl: "What do you call lonely cheese?"

Katelyn: "I don't know. What?"

Karl: "Provolone."

SING IT

Listener to the singer: "Don't forget your bucket."

Singer: "Why?"

Listener to the singer: "To carry your awful tune."

Chapter Five – Clean Jokes

COW
Q: What comes from a pampered dairy cow?

A: Spoiled milk.

BROOM
Q: Did you hear about the new kind of broom being sold right now?

A: Apparently, it's sweeping the nation!

DAD JOKES
Q: What do you call it when someone tells a dad joke but isn't a dad?

A: A faux pa.

Chapter Five – Clean Jokes

VOYAGE

Q: What happened when the red ship and blue ship collided in the Caribbean Sea.

A: All the survivors became marooned.

FIRE

Q: Did you hear the bad news about the big fire at the circus?

A: It was in tents.

JAIL

Q: What do people in jail use to call one another?

A: Cell phones.

Chapter Five – Clean Jokes

BREAKING THE LAW

Law enforcement apprehended 2 men holding a firecracker and a car battery.

They charged one while letting the other off.

HORSE AND PONY SHOW

Q: Why did the big horse hand the pony a cup of water?

A: Because the pony was a little horse!

WHALES

Q: What do you call a bunch of killer whales performing at the opera?

A: An Orca-stra!

Chapter Five – Clean Jokes

LAWYER JOKE

Darcy: "Do you know how lawyers say goodbye?"

Lance: "I don't know. How?"

Darcy: "We'll be suing ya."

MONTHS

Johnny: "Can February March?"

Janice: "No, but April May!"

BLOOD

A nurse asked me what type of blood I had.

I told her "Red."

FISHING

George: "What is your favorite way of watching a fishing tournament?"

Harry: "Live stream."

Chapter Six

DUMB GUY JOKES #2

BRAIN CELLS

Q: What do you call a dumb girl with only 2 brain cells?

A: Pregnant.

HELICOPTER

A dumb guy crashed his helicopter.

When the police asked him what he did to cause the crash, he said...

Dumb Guy: "I'm not sure. All I know is it got really cold, so I turned off the fan."

CONFUSION

Q: How do you confuse a dumb guy for hours?

A: Just print 'Turn Over' on both sides of a sheet of paper.

DUMBEST

Q: How can you identify the dumbest guy in the room?

A: He's the one that trips over the cordless phone.

DOUBTING

Q: What did the dumb girl think when the doctor told her she was pregnant?

A: I sure hope it's mine.

SOAKED

Q: What item becomes wet as it dries?

A: A towel!

Chapter Six - Dumb Guy Jokes #2

DOGNAPPING

A dumb guy was desperate for money and schemed to steal a dog and ask the owner for a ransom. So, he went to a neighbor's backyard, grabbed a dog, and said...

Dumb Guy: "I've dog-napped you."

Then he wrote a ransom note "I've kidnapped your dog. Leave $1,000 in a bag underneath the big oak tree in your backyard tomorrow by 10AM. Signed 'Dumb guy' "

The dumb guy taped the note to the dog's collar, then banged on the door of the house and ran away.

The following day the Dumb guy returned to see that, indeed, a bag was left under the oak tree. When he opened the bag, it had the $1,000 and a note that read, "I can't believe you did this to a fellow dumb guy."

Chapter Six - Dumb Guy Jokes #2

PIG

A woman strolls by a dumb guy on the side of the road that was holding a pig.

Woman: "Where did you get that thing?"

Pig: "I won him at the county fair."

TRACKS

3 dumb guys were out walking in nature when they came upon some tracks.

Dumb Guy #1: "Hey, look. Those are moose tracks."

Dumb Guy #2: "No, I think those are deer tracks."

And before the last dumb guy could say anything, the train hit them.

ALIENS

Q: What do an alien UFO and a dumb guy with a college degree have in common?

A: You may have heard of one, but you've never, ever seen one.

MILK ACCIDENT

Q: How did the dumb guy die while drinking milk?

A: Because the cow fell on him.

BEER

Q: How are a dumb guy and a bottle of beer the same?

A: They are both completely empty from the neck up.

DRIVING

Dumb guy: "I received a compliment on my driving today."

Friend: "From who?"

Dumb guy: " I don't know, but they left a paper on my windshield that read "Parking Fine."

Chapter Six - Dumb Guy Jokes #2

BUS STOP

Two dumb guys are sitting at a bus stop waiting for the bus.

The bus pulls up, and the door opens. Before getting on, one of the dumb guys asks the bus driver...

Dumb Guy #1: "Excuse me, will this bus take me to 12th street?"

The Bus Driver: "No, it won't."

After hearing this, the second dumb guy leans in and asks...

Dumb Guy #2: "Will it take ME to 12th street?"

COFFEE

Q: Why can't you give dumb guys coffee breaks at work?

A: Because it takes way too long to retrain them.

Chapter Six - Dumb Guy Jokes #2

SPEEDING

A dumb guy is speeding and gets noticed and stopped by a dumb cop.

The dumb cop approaches the car and asks for the dumb guy's license.

The dumb guy checks his wallet and discovers he doesn't have his license.

Dumb Cop: "Well, I need some ID. Can you give me anything else?"

The dumb guy checks his glove department and discovers a small mirror. He looks at it, then gives it to the dumb cop and says...

Dumb Guy: "Here, all I have is this picture of me."

The dumb cop grabs the mirror and also looks at it, and says,...

Dumb Cop: "Oh, I had no idea you were also a cop. Sorry about that, you can go."

GUNFIGHT

Q: How do you know a dumb guy tried to have an old western gunfight.

A: Because of all the bullet holes in the mirror.

Chapter Six - Dumb Guy Jokes #2

PRISON

A dumb woman is visiting her husband in prison.

When the dumb woman checks out, she tells one of the guards...

Dumb Woman: "You're making my husband work much too hard. He says he's exhausted!"

Laughing Guard: "What are you talking about? Your husband just eats and sleeps and hangs out all day and night in his cell."

Dumb Woman: "That's a lie. He just said to me that he's exhausted from digging that tunnel all month!"

Chapter Six - Dumb Guy Jokes #2

BLINKER

John was driving in his truck with his dumb guy friend.

John asked his dumb guy friend to stick his head outside his window to check if the truck's blinker was working.

So the dumb guy stuck his head out the window and said back to John,
Dumb Guy: "No, Yes, No, Yes, No, Yes, No..."

DEAD BIRD

A dumb guy and his girlfriend were walking in the park when the girlfriend stopped and looked down at the path.

Girlfriend: "Awww, look, a dead bird. How sad"

The dumb guy looks up at the sky and says...

Dumb Guy: "Dead bird, where?"

Chapter Six - Dumb Guy Jokes #2

KEYS

Two dumb guys walking back to the parking lot where their car was located.

Dumb guy #1: "Oh no, I locked the keys in the car."

Dumb guy #2: "Maybe I can try to unlock it using a coat hanger."

Dumb Guy #1: "Good idea, but hurry because it looks like it's gonna rain, and the top is down."

Chapter Six - Dumb Guy Jokes #2

FIRST DATE

A woman went on a first date with a dumb guy.

Dumb Guy: "Do you have any children?"

Woman: "Yes, I have one kid that's just under two."

Dumb Guy: "Hey, I might be kinda dumb, but even I know how many one is."

Chapter Seven

DAD JOKES #3

Har!
Har!
Har!

OLYMPICS

Q: What do Olympic sprinters eat before they race?

A: Not a thing, they fast!

GREENHOUSE

My new greenhouse was delivered.

I am so happy I wet my plants.

FRUIT WEDDINGS

Q: Why must melons always have weddings?

A: Because they cantaloupe!

ATOMS

Q: Why can't you ever trust atoms?

A: Because they make up everything.

WASHROOMS

Q: Why must you go to the bathroom if you're from Spain?

A: Because European.

SPACE MAN

Q: What is a space astronaut's favorite part of a keyboard?

A: The space bar, of course.

CYCLES

Q: What's the biggest difference between a man in a suit on a tricycle and a man dressed like a bum on a bicycle?

A: Attire!

GOAT

Q: What did the mountain goat father name his newborn son?

A: Cliff.

LEMONS

Q: How many lemons can grow on a lemon tree?

A: All of them!

ROCKERS

Lorne: "What did the rock band drummer name his twin daughters?"

Darrell: "I don't know. What?"

Lorne: "Anna one, Anna two!"

FAST MILK

Q: Why is milk the quickest liquid ever?

A: Because it's pasteurized before you get a look at it.

STAR WARS

Q: How did Darth Vader know what his son Luke Skywalker bought him for his birthday?

A: Because he felt his presents!

TASTY

Q: What is a magnificent spot for a taste bud?

A: Hmmm, I forgot... but it is on the tip of my tongue.

CHRISTMAS

Q: Are you having a hard time thinking about what to gift your friend for Christmas?

A: Buy him a fridge, then watch his face light up every time he opens it.

SUNSCREEN

Susan: "Do you know why bananas need good sunscreen?"

Charles: "No, I don't. Why?"

Susan: "Because they peel."

Chapter Seven - Dad Jokes #3

BUFFET

A chubby man at the buffet restaurant said, "I really, really want to go on a diet."

"Unfortunately, I have too much on my plate right now." Ha-ha

DAD JOKE

Haley: "Do you know why I like telling Dad jokes."

Sandra: "No, why?"

Haley: "Because every once in a while, he laughs!"

HOT WATER

Good-bye boiled water...

You will be mist.

Chapter Seven - Dad Jokes #3

STAIRS

Q: Why can't you ever trust stairs?

A: Because they're always up to something!

NAPPING CHAMP

I have become so darn good at napping that I can even do it with my eyes closed!

OFFICE

To the thief that stole my computer disc of Microsoft Office, I will get you.

You have my Word!

MOISTURE

If you are trying to get into the moisturizer business, the #1 tip I recommend is to apply daily.

Chapter Seven - Dad Jokes #3

ORANGE

Boris asked: "What rhymes with orange?"

Frank replied: "No, it doesn't!"

ZOMBIES

Q: What does a hungry zombie vegan eat?

A: "GRRRAAAIINS!"

SCISSORS

Q: What did the pair of scissors say to the paper?

A: "I don't like perforated lines because they're tearable."

GIGANTIC

Q: How do people talk to giants?

A: They use BIG words!

Chapter Seven - Dad Jokes #3

EYEBROWS

I told my best friend that she drew her eyebrows on much too high.

My friend seemed surprised!

NOSY PEPPER

Jose: "What does a very nosey pepper do?"

Stanley: "I don't know. What?"

Jose: "It gets jal-ap-eno business!"

FLAMINGO

Q: What do you do when your wife tells you to stop acting like a flamingo?

A: You put your foot down.

VOWELS

Q: What did one vowel say to the other vowel after it saved the first vowel's life?

A: "Aye, E! I owe you!"

BELIEF

Q: How is the Atheism belief structured?

A: As a non-prophet organization.

LAMP

Q: How did the woman feel when the thief stole her lamp?

A: She was delighted

MOTORCYCLES

Q: What sounds do witch's motorcycles produce?

A: "Broom Broom."

DINO NOISES

Q: Why can't you hear a pterodactyl dinosaur while using a toilet?

A: Because the P is silent.

PORTRAIT

Q: Why did the portrait get sent to prison?

A: Because it was framed.

HIPPIES

Jacob: "Do you know what to call a hippie's wife?

Kyle: "No, I don't. What?"

Jacob: "Mississippi."

BEARS

Q: What do you call a toothless bear?

A: A gummy bear, of course.

CONCERT

Q: Which performer's concert only costs 45 cents?

A: It's 50 Cent with Nickelback

KLEPTO

I suffer from kleptomania...

...and when it gets really bad, I have to take something for it.

WINNERS

George: "Why do winners always seem to win?"

Hank: "It beats me."

Chapter Seven - Dad Jokes #3

PRIEST

Q: How does the priest make holy water?

A: He boils the hell out of it. Ha-ha

RESIST

Q: Did you hear about the kid that refused to take her nap?

A: She was resisting a rest.

KISSES

Q: Why is it a bad idea to kiss anyone on January 1st?

A: Because it's only the first date. Ha-ha

WALLED

Q: What kind of wall saves a goal?

A: A D-'fence'!

ZIPPO VS HIPPO

Q: What's the difference between a zippo and a hippo?

A: One of them is very heavy, while the other is thinner and a little lighter.

FRIES

Q: Were French Fries first cooked in France???

A: No, they were actually cooked in Greece.

PIZZA

James: "Did you like my pizza joke?"

Karl: "No, I thought it was way too cheesy."

HOUSES

Dale: Do you know what a house wears?

Samuel: "No. What?"

Dale: "A dress."

BLACK AND WHITE

Q: What is white and black and white and black and white and black?

A: A Panda Bear in a revolving door.

TROPICAL

David: "I went on a tropical fruit diet but quit after just 1 month."

Jamie: "Why did you quit after only 1 month?"

David: "Trust me, eating only fruit will make any mango crazy."

Chapter Seven - Dad Jokes #3

BIRTHDAY CARDS

Yesterday I gave my dad his 60th birthday card.

He said just one would have been enough.

SEAFOOD

I had seafood for dinner yesterday,

Now I'm eel.

DAD BOD

Husband: "Oh, no! I think I have a 'dad bod'"

Wife: "That's ok, dear. Think of it more like it's a father figure."

JUNGLE

Q: Why did Tarzan of the jungle spend so much time at a golf course?

A: He was trying to perfect his swing!

Chapter Seven - Dad Jokes #3

WEIGHTS

Q: Why did the weight-lifter change his password?

A: Because he didn't think it wasn't strong enough!

Chapter Eight

CORNY JOKES

Chapter Eight - Corny Jokes

SO DUMB

Johnny: "Your friend is so dumb...."

Dale: "How dumb is he?"

Johnny: "Your friend is so dumb.....that when your mom said it was chilly outside, he ran out the front door with a spoon!"

BUGS

A girl asks his dad, "Dad, are bugs good to eat?" Dad: "That's rude. Please don't talk about disgusting things like that at the dinner table."

After eating, the father asks, "Daughter, why did you want to know about eating bugs?"

Daughter: "Oh, never mind. I saw that there was a fly in your soup, but it's gone now."

Chapter Eight - Corny Jokes

STAR WARS

If your name was Ella, and you married Darth Vader from Star Wars....then would your full name would now be Elevator???

TACOS

Q: Have you heard the new knock-knock jokes about the taco vendor?

A: They are really corny.

RACING

Q: What is the best way to win a race against vegetables?

Just get ahead of (the) lettuce!

COMPUTER FOOD

Q: What type of things do computers snack on?

A: Micro-chips.

Chapter Eight - Corny Jokes

ONIONS & BEANS

Q: What can you create with onions and baked beans?

A: Tear gas

GRASSHOPPER

A grasshopper sits down at the bar, and the bartender says, "Do you know there is a drink named after you!"

The grasshopper says, "You mean you have a drink named Frank?"

CORNY JOKE

Q: How do you describe this corny joke?

A: A maize zing!!!

FISH

Q: What type of fish do you show affection for?

A: A cuddlefish!

Chapter Eight - Corny Jokes

MERMAID

Q: What do you call a mermaid on top of a roof?

A: Aerial

NEBRASKA

Q: You wanna hear a joke about Nebraska?

...It's really corny.

DRY HUMOR

Q: Do you enjoy dry humor?

A: Because I have a good one about New Mexico!

CORNFIELD

Q: What did the dad say to his kids when they were walking in a cornfield?

A: "Watch out for stalkers."

TOILET PAPER

Frank: "Why couldn't the toilet paper cross the road?"

Sally: "I don't know. Why?"

Frank: "Because it got stuck in a crack." Ha-ha

SLICED BREAD

Q: Why wouldn't the 2 slices of bread speak to one another?

A: Because they had beef between them!

MONK

Q: Why couldn't the Tibetan monk sell his temple?

A: It had no monastery value.

Chapter Eight - Corny Jokes

FARM LIFE

Q: Why didn't people like the movie about life on a farm?

A: Because the plot was too corny and the picture quality was too grainy.

GHOSTS

Q: What do you call a Ghost that ran out of Boo's?

A: SOBER!

SMART SUN

Q: Why didn't the sun go to university?

A: Because it already had millions of degrees.

CHEDDAR POPCORN

Q: Why are jokes about cheddar popcorn so terrible

A: Because they're corny & cheesy.

Chapter Eight - Corny Jokes

MUSIC DJ

Q: What did the music DJ say to the vegetable farmer?

A: "Lettuce, turnip, the beet."

CORN STALK

Q: What did the stalk of corn say when all of its clothing came off?

A: "Oh, shucks."

CHIPS

Q: Wanna hear some jokes about tortilla chips?

A: Never mind, they're too corny.

CORNY JOKES

Q: To everyone that ever said they like corny jokes...

A: I'll give you an ear full.

Chapter Eight - Corny Jokes

SPEECH

Q: Before I gave my speech, I was going to tell a cereal joke

A: But it was much too corny, so I flaked.

KNOCK KNOCK!

"Who's there?"

"Frank Lee!"

"Frank Lee who?"

"Frank Lee my dear, I don't give a darn!"

TIGHT ROPE

Q: Why can't over-anxious people perform on a tight rope?

A: Because they're always too high-strung.

Chapter Eight - Corny Jokes

TRULY CORNY

Q: Do you know what is truly corny?

A: A field of corn, of course.

VEGETABLE FARMER

Q: What's a vegetable farmer's favorite type of joke?

A: A corny one.

Chapter Nine

DUMB GUY JOKES #3

SHOES

Q: Why do Dumb guys have "TGIF" printed on their shoes?

A: Toes go in first!

BABIES

A dumb guy and his wife were about to have a baby.

On the due date, the wife started having contractions, so the dumb guy took her to the hospital.

The dumb guy joined his wife in the delivery room for full support.

The wife gave birth to a girl and a boy.

The Dumb guy looked at his wife and said in a very mad tone...

Dumb Guy: "Wait a darn minute.....who the heck is the other father."

Chapter Nine - Dumb Guy Jokes #3

LOSING WEIGHT

A dumb guy is overweight, so his doctor puts him on a diet.

Doctor: "Please eat as you would normally for three days, then skip a day. Do this repeatedly for 1 month. When I see you after that 1 month, you should have lost about 5 pounds."

A month goes by, and the dumb guy goes back to the doctor.

Dumb guy: "Doctor, I lost 20 pounds."

Doctor: "That's incredible. And you followed my instructions?"

Dumb guy: "Yes, I did follow them. But I have to tell you, on the 4th day, I thought I was going to die."

Doctor: "Because you were that hungry?"

Dumb guy: "No, from skipping."

GLASS WALL

Samuel: "Why did the dumb guy climb the glass wall?"

David: "I don't know. Why?"

Samuel: "To see what was on the other side."

BANANAS

Q: How did the dumb guy get fired from his job at the banana plantation?

A: Because he kept throwing out all the bent ones.

DUMB GUY & GIRL

Q: How did the guy get a dumb girl to marry him?

A: He told her she was pregnant.

EGG

Q: What kind of egg did the very evil chicken lay?

A: A deviled egg! Haha

Chapter Nine - Dumb Guy Jokes #3

FIRST CLASS

A dumb guy boards a plane headed from New York to L.A. and sits down in a first-class seat. A flight attendant asks for his ticket, sees that it is an economy ticket, and asks him to move into the other section of the plane.

The Dumb guy refuses to move.

Other flight attendants also try to explain that he needs to move based on his ticket, yet he refuses.

After everyone has tried, they ask the Captain for assistance.

The Captain says, "I can solve this. My brother is a Dumb guy."

The Captain converses with the Dumb guy, and the Dumb guy eventually gets up and moves to his economy seat.

The amazed flight attendants ask the Captain how he managed to get the Dumb guy to move.

Captain: "Oh, it was easy. I just told him that first class wasn't flying to L.A."

DROWN

Q: How did the dumb guy nearly drown?

A: Someone told him there was a scratch 'n' sniff at the bottom of the swimming pool.

MECHANICS

2 dumb guys were talking about their cars.

Dumb guy #1: "My car is broken down. I need a mechanic."

Dumb guy #2: "You should use my mechanic. He's great."

Dumb guy #1: "Do you trust him? A lot of mechanics try to rip people off."

Dumb guy #2: "I was worried about that too, until my mechanic told me I need turn-signal fluid for my car, and only charged me ½ price."

CHEERIOS

Q: What did the dumb guy say when he was served Cheerios for breakfast?

A: "Yum, donut seeds."

CLOSET

Q: What do you call a dumb guy skeleton in a closet?

A: The winner of the Hide and Seek Championship from 1955

DISNEY WORLD

Two dumb guys decided to drive to Disney World.

On their way, they drove by a sign that read "Disney World - Left."

One dumb guy turned to the other and said, "Well, that's too bad. We might as well turn around and go back home."

Chapter Nine - Dumb Guy Jokes #3

SMARTPHONE
Q: What is it called when a dumb guy uses a smartphone?

A: Artificial Intelligence.

FIREMEN
Q: What types of crackers do firemen mix into their soup?

A: Firecrackers!

FISHY
Q: How do you call a fish?

A: You drop it a line!

TRIANGLE
Q: What did the triangle shout at the circle to hurt its feelings?

A: You're pointless!

Chapter Nine - Dumb Guy Jokes #3

TELEVISION, PLEASE

A dumb guy visits a store and discovers a real bargain.

Dumb guy: "Hello, I'd like to buy this TV, please."

Salesman: "Sorry, I can't sell this to you. You are too dumb."

The dumb guy was angry and thought he'd get back at the salesman for calling him dumb. So he went home, changed into a suit and tie, and returned to the store.

Dumb guy: " Hello, I'd like to buy this TV, please."

Salesman: " Sorry, I can't sell this to you. You are too dumb."

The dumb guy, mad as ever, wanted to get back at that Salesman even more, so he returned home, cut his hair, put on nerdy glasses, grabbed a pipe mimicking what a brilliant professor would look like, then returned to the store.

Dumb guy: Hello, I'd like to buy this TV, please."

Chapter Nine - Dumb Guy Jokes #3

Salesman: Sorry, I can't sell this to you. You are too dumb."

Dumb guy: "I demand to talk to you, manager."

The manager comes by, and the dumb guy says to the manager....

Dumb guy: Hello, I'd like to buy this TV, please."

Manager: "Are you dumb or something? That's a microwave."

HIGH-5

Q: How does a dumb guy high-5?

A: He smacks himself in the forehead.

FISH

Q: How does a dumb guy drown a fish?

A: He holds it underwater!

DANGER

2 dumb guys shared an apartment.

Dumb guy #1: "I heard on the news that 90% of accidents occur in the home."

Dumb guy #2: "Then we should move."

Chapter Nine - Dumb Guy Jokes #3

PROUD

Q: Why was the dumb guy so darn proud of himself?

A: Because he completed a puzzle in 3 hours, and the box reads "4-8 years".

BAR LIMIT

18 dumb guys were lined up outside a bar but wouldn't go in.

The sign on the door read "21+ only".

CONSTIPATED

Q: Have you gone to the new movie, "Constipated?"

A: No? Because it hasn't come out yet!

FLIES

Q: What do you call insects flying around inside a dumb guy's head?

A: Space Invaders.

Chapter Ten

SUPER JOKES

Chapter Ten - Super Jokes

YOGA

Q: In yoga, what do you call the heavy breaths people take while holding a pose?

A: Yoga pants.

BEACH

Q: What is the best beach day?

A: Sunday, of course!

PRETZEL

Q: What is a pretzel's favorite dance move?

A: The Twist.

MUSHROOM

Q: Why should you invite mushrooms to parties?

A: Because they are such fungi! Har-har-har

CHICKENS

Q: How do chickens cheer for their sports team?

A: They egg them on!

DAYS OF THE WEEK

Q: When does Thursday come before Wednesday?

A: In the dictionary!

BIRDIE

Q: Why did the little birdie go to the doctor?

A: To get a tweetment

Chapter Ten - Super Jokes

BODY PARTS

Q: What has 1 foot, 1 head and 4 legs?

A: A Bed

COMPUTER

Q: Where did the computer go to listen to music and dance?

A: To the disc-o

WETTEST

Q: Why is England the wettest of all countries?

A: Because Queen Elizabeth has reigned there for years!

PRUNES

Q: Why did Peter ask out a prune?

A: Because he couldn't find a date!

Chapter Ten - Super Jokes

DRIVERS

Q: Who makes money driving their customers away?

A: An Uber driver

SHOOT

Q: What do you shoot killer bees with?

A: A bee-bee gun

CALENDAR

Q: What happened to the guy who stole a calendar?

A: He got 12 months.

CANDY

Q: What do you call something sweet that was stolen?

A: Hot chocolate!

Chapter Ten - Super Jokes

CHICKEN

Q: Where do they sell chicken broth in bulk?

A: The Stock Market

WINNIE

Q: What did Winnie The Pooh say to his acting agent?

A: "Show me the honey!"

UP AND OVER

Q: What goes up & over hills, through towns, but doesn't ever move?

A: A road!

DOG RACING

Q: What type of dogs like racing of any kind?

A: Lap dogs

Chapter Ten - Super Jokes

THUNDER

Q: When do you see thunder and lightning in a science lab?

A: When scientists are brainstorming!

PIRATES

Q: Why couldn't the pirates play card games?

A: Because the captain was sitting on the deck!

MONKEY

Larry: "What do you call a baby monkey?"

Frank: "I don't know. What?"

Larry: "A Chimp off the old block."

Chapter Ten - Super Jokes

ELEPHANT FISH

Q: What do you get when you mix an elephant and a fish?

A: Swimming trunks.

BLANKET

Johnny: "What did the blanket say to the bed?"

Peter: "I Don't know. What?"

Johnny: "Don't worry, I've got you covered!"

Chapter Ten - Super Jokes

BIRDIES

Q: What type of bird sticks to everything?

A: A Vel-Crow

CLOCKS

Gail: "What did the new digital clock say to the old grandfather clock?"

Sara: "I don't know, what?"

Gail: "Look grandpa, no hands!" Ha-ha.

ARMY MONTHS

Q: Which month do army soldiers hate the most?

A: March!

Chapter Ten - Super Jokes

DENTIST

Hank: "What did the judge say to the dentist?"

Sally: "I don't know. What?"

Hank: "Do you swear to pull the tooth, the whole tooth and nothing but the tooth."

LETTERS

Q: What starts with P, ends with E, and has millions of letters in it?

A: "Post Office!"

STATES

Q: Which U.S. State has the tiniest soft drinks?

A: Mini-soda

OCTOPUS

Q: How does an octopus go to war?

A: Well Armed

Chapter Ten - Super Jokes

TEA

Q: What type of tea is hard for people to swallow?

A: Reality

FOOD

Q: Why was the woman looking for food on her friend?

A: Her friend said "dinner is on me."

CAMERA

Q: What do you call a crazy, out of control camera?

A: A loose Canon.

Chapter Ten - Super Jokes

CAT BURGLAR

Q: Did you hear about the over-sensitive cat-burglar?

A: Apparently, he takes things personally.

SMOKER

Q: Did the smoker get everything she wanted for her birthday?

A: Clothes, but no cigar.

BAKER

Q: How do you impress a baker's daughter on a first date?

A: Bring her flours.

YOGURT

Q: Why did the yogurt visit the museum?

A: Because it was cultured.

Chapter Ten - Super Jokes

TOMATO

Gale: "Why did the tomato turn all red?"

Karl: "I don't know. why?"

Gale: "Because it saw the salad dressing!"

CANS

Q: Why did John not like his can crusher job?

A: He said it was soda pressing.

BEES

Q: Where do bees wait for public transit?

A: At a buzz stop!

COPS

Q: What did the cop say to his own sweater?

A: "Do you know why I pulled you over?"

CHICKEN

Q: What part of a chicken is the most musical?

A: The drumstick

Chapter Eleven

YUK-YUK JOKES

Chapter Eleven - Yuk-Yuk Jokes

MAGIC FISHERMAN

Q: What did the magic fisherman say before performing a trick?

A: "Pick a cod, any cod!"

SESAME SEED

Q: Why didn't the sesame seed stop betting on horse races?

A: Because he was on a roll.

YEAST

Q: Why did the broke baker sell yeast?

A: To raise some dough.

SNAILS

Q: How do snails settle disagreements?

A: They slug it out.

Chapter Eleven - Yuk-Yuk Jokes

PENGUINS

Q: Why can't boy penguins ask out girl penguins?

A: Because they can't break the ice.

DIFFERENCES

Q: What's the difference between ignorance and apathy?

A: "Don't know! Don't care!"

HAMBURGERS

Q: Where do hamburgers go for music and dancing?

A: To the meat-ball.

BELT

Q: Why was the belt sent to jail?

A: It held up a pair of pants!

Chapter Eleven - Yuk-Yuk Jokes

BEARS

Q: What do you call a bear not wearing any socks?

A: Bare-foot.

SERVED

Q: What can you serve but cannot eat?

A: A volleyball.

SUGAR

Q: Why did the girl spread sugar on her bed before going to sleep?

A: She wanted to have sweet dreams.

Chapter Eleven - Yuk-Yuk Jokes

HIPSTER

Q: How did the hipster burn his tongue from his chai-latte with half-foam?

A: He drank it before it was cool!

FOREST

Q: How do crazy people walk through the forest?

A: By taking the psycho path.

CODE

Q: What is an apology written in only dots and dashes?

A: Remorse code.

YELLOW

Q: What's yellow in color and moves up and down?

A: A banana in an elevator.

Chapter Eleven - Yuk-Yuk Jokes

RESTAURANT

Q: What walks into a restaurant, eats shoots, and leaves?

A: A Panda

GHOSTS

Q: What type of streets do ghosts haunt most often?

A: Dead ends!

CHURCH

Q: What do you call it when Batman purposely skips out on church?

A: Christian Bale

Chapter Eleven - Yuk-Yuk Jokes

BOOKMARK

Yesterday, my niece asked, "Can you hand me a bookmark?" and I became worried.

15 years old and she still can't remember my name is Peter.

BATTERY

Terrance: "I picked up a bunch of dead car batteries yesterday."

Olivia: "Did that cost a lot of money?"

Terrance: "No, they were free of charge."

STORE

I went to the corner store yesterday.... bought all four corners.

SECRET SERVICE

The secret service stopped yelling "Get down!" when President Trump was in office. Instead, they shouted, "Donald, duck!"

NOSTALGIA

Nostalgia, it just isn't what it used to be.

LANGUAGE

Q: Do you know what the least spoken language in the entire world is?

A: Sign language, of course.

Chapter Eleven - Yuk-Yuk Jokes

PIRATES

Q: What are the pirates of the Caribbean?

A: 1 slice of blueberry pie is $4.50 in Jamaica, and $5.50 a slice in the Bahamas.

PSYCHIATRIST

During my last session, my psychiatrist said to me,

Psychiatrist: "Cheer up, Brian. Your situation could be worse. Imagine if you were trapped underground alone in a large hole filled with water."

I know she meant well.

Chapter Eleven - Yuk-Yuk Jokes

FAT KNIGHT

Walter: "Who was the absolute fattest knight of King Arthur's round table?"

Peter: "I don't know. Who?"

Walter: "Sir Cumference. And he gained all his size from too much pi."

TIGERS

Q: Why do jungle tigers have stripes?

A: So they don't get spotted!

CAR

Q: What do you call a retired Marine in a Chevy sports car?

A: A Corps vet in a Corvette.

Chapter Eleven - Yuk-Yuk Jokes

MOTHER

Wife: "As I held our daughter with 1 arm and opened the door with the other, I thought, 'How would 1-armed mothers do this?"

Husband: "Single-handedly."

JUSTICE

Norm: "You know, they say justice is the dish best served cold."

Mason: "Maybe, but if it were served hot, it would be justwater."

LOOK

Margaret: "How do I look?"

Danny: "Duh, with your eyes."

Chapter Eleven - Yuk-Yuk Jokes

BELT

Justine: "What do you call a belt with a watch on it?"

Katherine: "I don't know, what?"

Justine: "A waist of time!"

FROGGIE

Q: What is a frog's favorite thing to drink?

A: Croak-a-cola! Har-d-har-har.

INSECTS

Q: What insects are great at counting?

A: Account-ants!

Chapter Eleven - Yuk-Yuk Jokes

TOASTER

Q: I wanted a brand-new toaster, but the store website was too annoying....

A: It had too many pop-ups!

FONTS

Q: Times New Roman and Comic Sans walk into a bar.

A: You two can get out!" says the bartender. "I don't serve your type here!"

FARMER

Q: What did the farmer tell the cow when the cow wouldn't go to sleep?

A: "Hey, it's past-ure bedtime!"

Chapter Eleven - Yuk-Yuk Jokes

REPTILES

Q: What did ancient reptiles get instead of blisters?

A: Dino sores!

POTATO

Q: How do potatoes solve their arguments?

A: They hash it out.

Chapter Eleven - Yuk-Yuk Jokes

CONSTRUCTION

Q: What nails do construction workers hate hammering?

A: Fingernails

WET

Q: What is the wettest of all animals?

A: The rain-deer!

PILLOWS

Q: Have you heard about those corduroy pillows?

A: Because they're making head-lines!

SPORTS CAR

My Boss drove in to work with a brand-new sports car.

Me: "That's a beautiful car. It must be expensive. I would love to own something like that one day."

Boss: "Thanks. It is expensive. And you know, if you keep working hard, put in those hours, maybe...just maybe I can buy an even better one next year."

Chapter Twelve

MORE CARTOONS

CREDITS

ILLUSTRATIONS

Each and every Illustration(s) are paid for and fully licensed with permission for commercial use from copyright holder - artist Ron Leishman and toonaday.com

Information sources

All jokes included in this publication are original or rewritten from legendary classics, public domain – were used for authenticity. No joke included is a direct copy. Any and all sources below provided subject material, reference, and inspiration and all contain changed copy.

funnyjokes.com

bestjokehub.com

jokes.lol

worstjoke.com

funnydadjokes.com

quicklyseek.com

directhit.com

parade.com

topfunnyjokes.com

wickeduncle.co.uk

punsandoneliners.com

jokesoftheday.net

CONGRATULATIONS
YOU FINISHED

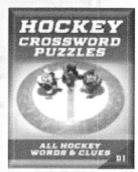

Made in the USA
Las Vegas, NV
18 December 2023

83138419R00115